A PALETTE OF LEAVES

3-8-2013

For Jeff,
Fellow artist and creative spirit—

With thanks for your great help
and support for my art.
Best wishes,
Elythe

A PALETTE OF LEAVES

Poems by Edythe Haendel Schwartz

Edythe Haendel Schwartz

MAYAPPLE PRESS 2012

Published by   MAYAPPLE PRESS
362 Chestnut Hill Rd.
Woodstock, NY 12498
www.mayapplepress.com

ISBN 978-1-936419-14-2

ACKNOWLEDGMENTS

California Quarterly: In Edward Hopper's *Western Motel*, Reprieve, Omelet; *Calyx:* Help Wanted: Bra Fitter, Apricot Crisp; *Cave Wall:* My Father's Pipe, Sport; *Cider Press Review:* At the Paper Sculpture Exhibit (as Closed Out by Scale,) An Encounter with Cy Twombly at The Whitney; *Earth's Daughters:* At Thunder Hole, Dragonfly, Eat/Fast; *Friends of Acadia Journal:* A Natural Phenomenon; *JAMA:* Habañera, The Conchologist and the Shoemaker, Lacunae; *J Journal:* Pantoum for the World Cup; *Kaleidoscope:* At the River, Still; *Vermont Literary Review:* Legacy; *Natural Bridge:* Resilience; *Passager:* Blues for Dorothy; *Pearl:* Hands, Does It Hurt?; *Persimmon Tree:* Resist; *PMS—poemmemoirstory:* Alice Neel Speaks; *Poetica:* Chromatic Alphabet; *Poet Lore:* After Mama's Stroke; *The Potomac Review:* The Astronomer; *Runes Review:* Edward Weston's *Pepper*; *Sierra Nevada Review:* Calimari en Su Tinta; *Spire:* At the River; *Spillway:* From Behind the Pane I Watch Her; *Suisun Valley Review:* Five Degrees Fahrenheit, Still; *Thema:* Accident, Maryland; *Water-Stone Review:* Alice Neel Paints *Futility of Effort*; *Yale Journal for Humanities in Medicine:* Biopsy.

"A Natural Phenomenon" won first prize in the *Friends of Acadia 2012* Poetry Competition. "Resist" was a winner in Persimmon Trees Western States Fall, 2011 Poetry Competition. "Exposure" was an award winner in *The Anna Davidson Rosenberg Awards for Poems on the Jewish Experience, 2007*, and was first published on the JCCSF web site, www.jccsf.org. "The Painter at Ninety-One" appears in the Anthology, *Still Going Strong: Memoirs, Stories, and Poems about Great Older Women*, Haworth Press, 2006. "Long Odds" appears in the anthology, *No Place for A Puritan: Literature of The California Desert*, Heyday Books, 2009. "Habanera" appears in the anthology *Honoring Motherhood*, Skylight Paths, 2008. "Suspension" appears in the anthology *Connections: New York City Bridges in Poetry*, P and Q Press, 2012. The following poems first appeared in my chapbook, *Exposure*, Finishing Line Press, 2007: Care, The Body Project, Still Water, Suspension, Cleaning Out Her Closet, Revelation (as Chromatic,) *La Guerre et La Paix (*as Françoise Gilot Tells Picasso *You Must Paint Peace,*) and Rafting.

I would like to thank Joshua Mckinney for his ongoing support and friendship, Bob Stanley and Connie Gutowsky for feedback and friendship, and Sy Schwartz for his close reading of my poems, encouragement, care, and always, joyous partnership.

Cover art *Festival* by Edythe Haendel Schwartz. Cover designed by Judith Kerman. Book designed and typeset by Amee Schmidt with titles in Myriad Pro and text in Adobe Caslon Pro. Author photo courtesy of Sy Schwartz.

CONTENTS

ONE

TWO

THREE

For Sy

ONE

ALICE NEEL PAINTS *FUTILITY OF EFFORT*

Oil on canvas, 1930

I've drawn the small figure in meager space,
in lost light, colorless, her face
twisted, her head caught
between the bed posts.

I read about it in the paper—
her mother was in the kitchen
ironing. I've drawn a hanging
line, a fragile vertical
to slice the canvas, the girl
strangled by chance

the way my daughter was.
Diptheria took her,
the white threads webbing her
throat, choking off air. No care
could cut the fever, care no weapon
against the viscous membrane. A brush

of fate so fast and dark, lamp black, ochre
and in a corner hovering, one eye
a paralyzing stare, no eye
to see, and where her
mouth would be, no breath
to draw.

CALIMARI EN SU TINTA

As if this very drawing could help her
survive, my daughter fists the blue
marker, flecks the bush she scribbles.

Blueberries she says, trusting
my hand.

I remember that night in Madrid
before she was born
when we ordered squid in its own ink.
How we stared at the plate, the black
stain spreading, the dead
animal lying in its own pool, no tool
against harm,

the way my daughter's arm now lies
on the page, while lymphocytes fail
under the drawn surface.
Then, I didn't know what it meant
to sink *en su tinta.*

                   She draws
away from me.

Exposure

New York, July, 1949

Prologue

The city's flow sunders.
Animosities flare
in small rooms, rumors seep below
door lintels, slow air—
the illness closes breath. No one knows
what to look for. No one can block
the fear. Some conceal children,
legs lank as marionettes. Mothers lie
when power knocks.
Some say, with illness comes poison
to justify—

I

The city says *Stay put. Stay in.* We seal
windows, the little ones so hot and wet
they look as though they had been dipped
in oil. And now my neighbor's girl,
lungs stuck together like a wad of gum
on the sole, body's bellows with no hum—
whisked out of her mother's arms
and left alone, a sterile hospital bed, her doll,
Miss Nancy, burned, her red shoes,
burned, child's world gone in a flash,
parents trapped behind a wall of glass,
like touching ice—

the girl encased, iron lung whooshing in
and out each breath against death, riven.

II

All day my Solomon presses on the window
watching the forbidden street. Sun

shrouds the dust. He aches to swim and run.
I keep him in. He's hot, not sick. *Polio*
I tell him. *Swimming pools are closed,
better you should breathe hot air than fever.*
He sinks against my flesh, my prayer,
smells stewing chicken steaming up my clothes.

His father stitches suits downtown, rides the subway
hanging by a handstrap, fifty dollars
a week when there is work—   worn out by
little pay, puts some aside for drink, his collars
shredding at the seams. I can't stop
the corrosion in his gut.

III

So disregard the news, the will
of God? No exodus for us. Abe yells
I shouldn't scare, but we are prey.
Isolation rules. The smell of boiled wool
raises the terror of burned limbs.
My *Tateh* should only know—
We dreamed American; tomorrow
we might be victims.

Tonight, Shabos. Flour dusts my fingers
as I knead the dough for challah.
Abe will hide inside the paper

but tonight I'll keep my mind
on Solomon, the light without the dark,
my hands above the candles—

STILL WATER

There must be a reason
why I've put her there

            a speck

in the middle of a sea,
head a spread of madder, cap a daub of thalo blue.

I thought she might find solitude
in buoyancy, the vastness of canvas.

I've brushed her in no bigger than a comma,

where yellow strokes the break
            between cerulean and gray,
far from the swell and boom
          of surf
her children skylarking
on sand   invisible

        she needs to stay
where I've put her
     still water on the surface,
and below,
      the movement slow as morning
              prayer.

There she cannot smell the baby oil,
sunscreen, salt, cannot hear the cries

of vendors selling leis. Moored
off the horizon, she hears only

unheard melodies.

When a sodden cloud empties with a loud clap
of thunder, will her colors bleed?

RESIST

In the cloth I see the ghost
of the artist I once knew
who coveted
the cobalt blue Giotto loved.

A residue of wax
pocks the silk, plants illusion—
some vision of what lies
ahead.

No congruence. The fabric falls
in folds the way a head
of lettuce
comes undone

the hues in layers
as if strata
of conscious and unconscious
matter.

Today, even the green is tinged with grey,
the shadows heavy on my hands, dye
deepening like slime
in the kitchen sink I forgot to clean.

I must let the blues evolve,
the spirals of the iris sorrow
the surface
like furrows on my face.

How I wrestle this sentence
fixed in wax, this dye my wary
hand imposes on the silk; steam
hisses from the iron,

this ghost I press and press—

IN EDWARD HOPPER'S *WESTERN MOTEL*...

1957, Yale Museum of Art

A lone woman in a plum dress
stares from the edge
of a bed. Sunlit fingers press
against the wooden frame.

Her bed is clean. Silence strains
the glacial surface of her face. The pane
deepens distance, hills mauve and umber.
The man behind the easel has made her

with a brush of amber on a swept-back do—
no muss; sharp light creases her chin.
How deeply drawn the lines
that hold her place—

Surely my mother must have known
such lines—   her hand-drawn generations
of drosophila wing mutations, hidden.
I see her in our midcentury kitchen

slicing hearts of romaine to calm
the arugula, eyes longing
to dissect again, the weight
of fingers restless on the knife.

From Behind the Pane I Watch Her

shinny up the beech,
no sound but the soft crack of branch

where her kite is caught. Feet
trust the bough will not break when she frees

the tail, unknots the line. How swiftly
fingers ease the twine, release the snag; the agony

is mine alone. Dusk. So hard to see
where tree becomes child or child becomes tree.

AT THE RIVER

Small hands drift
in shallows, riffle iridescence

       flash
       on father's line

trout swishing
like the teardrop gown
her mother wears
to bed
       brown satin
flecked with wine.

The child trembles, stares
            as father reels

the rainbow, whacks
it hard against a rock.

The fish has no arms,
can't raise hands
against the blow.

LACUNAE

Mistletoe haloes the dead
oak standing in the park,
empty as a child unfed.

The plant clings to bark
living only on what's left,
oak standing in the park,

yet empty, only its cloak left,
lightning charred inside—
like a child living on what's left

of chipped self may hide
in skin, hoping you will hold
her, not strike. She burns inside,

an oak standing, growing old
too soon from fending blows
on skin, hoping you will hold

her snug against you, fill hollows
the way Mistletoe haloes the dead
oak. No hope of ending blows,
she grows empty, a child unfed.

THE BODY PROJECT

At fourteen Naomi resembled a pear—
faced the table carefully
the bowl of buttered popovers
releasing steam.

She needed to taste
the care

hidden in the yeast
the feast unyielding

the table always set
for someone else—

Her mother loved her

cleverness

boasted *my daughter, gifted*
able to toss a French omelet
fill us all with sweet
aroma roasted garlic and thyme
and still get A's—

Hard to know
when Naomi began to pare
down wanting
to be
barely there
a shell

tempered and translucent

Now too tired to swallow air   she cracks
eggs, fills the bowl with froth

yellow chiffon
that scarf
with which she used to dance—

CARE

He wants to strike
symptoms,

plum colored urine
milky skin.

He needs to pass
this test.

He wants to run.
He's only twenty one, losing
equilibrium.

He works weekends tending bar at Harlows.

       Music out of tune. Riffs circulate,

trumpet a future
       with improvisation. Like infection—

Apricot Crisp

After chemotherapy, she bakes.
Riven body pressed against the sink,
she washes apricots. Water soothes
her stiffened fingers as she frees
each stone, so easily removed she cannot
help but laugh. The smell of ripening
induces floating images of daughters
barefoot in the kitchen, chopping fruit,
their little fingers stained with juice.
Alone, she listens to her breathing
stumble over tumors,
layers crescent moons of apricots,
flutes the crust.

LEGACY

A talc miner's daughter speaks

They dug a vein below the mountain,
a seam of wealth
called Talc, from *talq*, Arabic for talk,
but there, no talk, the men in the mine
masked as they struck the fibrous mass.

I remember my father
coming out of darkness, his eyes
squinting with grit
and talc mossing his nostrils, paper mask
never enough where bad air
followed the veins of ore—

Talc greyed my father's skin, spread
into flesh, the darkness never leaving
him; his arms smelled of earth, while above
women dusted scented talcum on their breasts.

Tongue stalled at home, my father sat
on the naugahyde lounger, his lips numb
with tobacco and talc, his body shifting
only to flick an ash—

BIOPSY

I am not supposed to bleed.
The doctor probes for tissue, a patch

of cells small as the button on my vintage
satin blouse,

cells greedy as a child wanting
chocolate—   *a spot*

of concern, she says. Stirrups
brace my feet. Facing up

to questions, my closed throat
like a hard birth, I try to give voice

with caught breath. I want
myself at twenty, ready to offer

nourishment to some future
child who would cry *more, more*—her

lexicon at two, too small to name things by,
that child I am looking for.

Wit's what's needed. *Just twenty
seconds more*, the doctor says.

She reminds me of the woman
who fitted my first diaphragm

fifty years before
when all I wanted was love.

AFTER HER STROKE

Shawled in silence,
she parts her lips,
lifts a hand as though the hand
could heal the tongue.
Lost, the names of things
she once found easily, her fluency
a rise and fall of breath, words and laughter
rushing forth like wind.

Aphasia slips between us, vowels
and consonants divorced from sense.
White hair sifts across her eyes,
pupils dark with scraps of memories.
I stroke her skin, translucent tissue
tracing where she's been.
She spits the syllable *bu,* and takes a breath.
Tongue lifted by desire, she rolls the sounds,
My kin der you er beau ti full,
triumph blushing on her face.

HANDS

The hands that held the charcoal, pencil, brush,
the burnt sienna, prussian blue, unfold to scrub

the paint no longer there, the yellow
that could tremble as wind torments a daffodil—

collages she called *merz*—bits of old letters
her fingertips would work into the clean colors

so that hues were muffled as if pulled
from a world of nuances—the way she'd said

she once rubbed spoons with mother's silver cloth
to rid them of color, mother severe

about tarnish, how she would skate on the thin ice
of her mother's house, glide on the rims of glasses—

Always now, find her
in the rocker, days her fingers discover

the edge, tap tap tap on the drum table
with its hidden drawer of scrabble

as if tapping would uncover
who she was—some scarlet, some ochre.

Now only a blank nod—her hands clock
hours in pockets of her painter's smock,

the cotton stained alizarin and violet,
hues that would document the last

hand she could lift against the growing black.

MY FATHER'S PIPE

A little yellow to warm the bowl, the teacher said.
I drew my father's pipe, image and ground a web
of prismacolor: carmine, raw umber. *A little yellow*—
that hue I could not swallow

sallow as my father's skin, though his beloved
pipe was not his Lucifer—radiation that, *White
Sands*, white light, sun disk, fireball tongued
with glister, incandescence in the *Tularosa*—

uranium, unleashed. I filled my father's pipe
with burnt sienna, ignited flakes viridian
and copper, saw the plume—mind's eye
flash on rod and cone, feathers of fume

rising in the ether, augury unknown, shadow
on a scan the body's residue of that false dawn—
the marrow making no more red, the puking
in a hospital bowl. *A little yellow to warm*

the bowl, the teacher said. I drew as if the sun
might fail to rise one day, the earth drawn
into a black hole; my fingers measured
my father's time, the right hue out of reach.

Two

Rafting

Where the Limay flows pewter
through the Patagonian Steppes, eases
its way below terminal moraine, weaves
between islands held firm by tree roots, new
land follows the only plan it can, where
eons back earth slipped, left cliff foot
in sediment, life trapped in amber—
traces of cycad stems, borings
of beetles, where in the raft
this afternoon, a father voices over
river roar, *we must toss a child in*
to lighten the load—everybody laughs
and what's to come, the raft pitching
and rolling in a stretch of white water.

Along the slope of the moraine,
a trail winds and a boy coils behind
eroded basalt columns etched with lichens,
waits to hurl thistle grenades at rafters
coming down river, his need seething
through cracks, the boy thrust at the margin
of earth's racket.

This morning, a thrush died in the mouth
of my son's golden retriever, a brief shiver
of wings, then fell back in grass only to be
retrieved and tossed again while the children
licked their fill of popsicles, *frambuesa*
red juice staining chins, and here,
here, watching sun shatter basalt and shadow
boulders of the tertiary, I understand why,

after the tilting of plates sliding under
oceans and continents, sutures slipped
and slip again, San Andreas, Great Rift Valley,
Himalayan Scarp, why, after rock was sculpted
into river bed by the last receding glacier
bringing us to time present, equilibrium shifts
and shifts again.

Hills speckle with Amancay,
Lupine, Verbena, and Creosote broken only by
prism of azure, verdigris, and the water ouzel,
slate dipper bobs a shape on the river, head under,
only yellow webs facing up

to sun in the boat's wake, no life extinct except
naturalmente, no life lost by intention
until massacres left corpses littering this cut
in the moraine. Massacres: what the Argentines
did to the Mapuche of Patagonia, Columbus
to the Arawaks of the Bahamas, Cortés to the Aztecs
of Mexico, Pizarro to the Incas of Peru, the English
settlers of Virginia and Massachusetts to the Powhatans
and Pequots, and ahead, the far shore draws my mind
to the American where sun and stars slip backwards
this season, hemisphere where I began.

I see the current accelerate, see bright rips whisper
up in whirlpools, leave footnotes of upheaval, bones
of snake and crow, ghosts of auroch, mastadon, and human,
seeds of locoweed—here, this river, the Limay
where our raft scrapes a rock bowl
marked with a cross, and the father taunts—
two children drowned by those rocks, bodies eaten
by sharks. You're lying, says the boy. *There are no sharks*
in rivers. The father grabs the boy's waist, says
toss a child overboard, the raft has too much weight
and everybody laughs—

Pantoum for the World Cup

After Eduardo Galeano's Soccer in Sun and Shadow

A boy heads the ball in sun and shadow.
Twelve pesos slide off the edge of his hand.
He wears Adidas soccer cleats
inscribed by *Ronaldinho*.

Twelve pesos slide off the edge of his hand,
two hundred an hour for the field of false turf
where boys in cleats inscribed by *Ronaldinho*
kick and run. Others play on spits of sand.

Two hundred an hour for the field of false turf
near avenues that curve into suburbs
where boys kick and run. Others play on spits of sand
beside a car-choked Buenos Aires highway

miles from avenues that curve into suburbs.
Old Fiats rattle by, drown out the shouts of *GOL*
beside a car-choked Buenos Aires highway
rank with *omnibus* exhaust.

Old Fiats rattle by, drown out the shouts of *GOL*.
Back and forth the boys run barefoot
breathing *omnibus* exhaust.
The ball bends the air.

Back and forth the boys run barefoot
on spaces not devoured by building run amok—
The ball bends the air
and grownups cheer for boys who score a goal

on spaces not devoured by building run amok.
Boys dream of being *Ronaldinho*.
Grownups cheer for boys who score a goal,
boys who head the ball in sun and shadow.

STILL

I watch the children bury dolls
in shoebox beds, bodies wrapped
in rags. Through the window

thunderclouds split sense, beat
hard the house's bones, behead
young mums.

How easily a fracture
in the weather clears the air,
this air my children breathe, still sweet.

Across the sea, children catch
cross-fire, lie like crumpled cloth,
limbs akimbo

where men and women charged
with handiwork of blood,
        turn laughter into stone.

What do the children know,
the way they twist the limbs from dolls,
shield play in whispering, heads bowed
        as if in prayer?

FIVE DEGREES FAHRENHEIT

Afghanistan, Winter

Daybreak in the killing
frost. A man waves
from a makeshift platform

      at the out of focus sea
      of faces flattened
      by the telephoto lens.

Behind the camera's eye:

      A mother holds her cold-
      hardened baby, three days old,

      his blanket in shreds, her mouth
      agape as if to bare a sore
      tooth.

      An AK 47 leans
      against her
      tent. Hanging
      from the rifle's butt, a child's sock.

      A father feeds his children
      Opium

                exposure lengthens.

GLASS BANQUET

After Beth Lippman's Bancketje, Renwick Gallery,
Smithsonian American Art Museum, Washington, D.C.

A glass rests upside down
its rim silent

the grand table laden
with bowls of crystal grapes,
see-through pears—   whole

or broken

crowded by platters of fowl
and fish—   heads whole
or half eaten, bones cracked

or bitten

400 pieces of glass
set before us—   a feast of glass
so transparent we see ourselves

exposed—

EAT/FAST

Morning
I will eat only this
one soft-cooked egg,
the yolk, a sun spooned slowly
to my mouth.
Later, half a grapefruit,
ruby flesh torn free
by sawteeth on a silver spoon,
sweet and bitter on my tongue.
At dusk, one fish,
a baby rainbow trout,
quick-broiled, blistered
near its eyes that dare me
eat and eat and eat.
I dream of salmon
bathed in grenadine, thick syrup
darkening its flesh, pasta
tossed with lavender and cream,
Tiramisu.
Awake, I hear the beat of hunger
as a dirge, voices mourning
Such a pretty face

JULY 1943

New York

It was a time our mothers huddled under
radio static, strained to hear
reporting from the front, transmission

stutter drowned by thunder as rain stared down,
refused to clear the air, everyone wanting
release, like the pauses you could hear

at Mintons uptown, where Dizzy blew
his angled horn. Sometimes voices wrangled
over schemes for making do, the menfolk far

from home; sometimes, silence, mothers wringing
hands on aprons, wiping sweat from dreams,
the only waterfall that summer, a jimmied fireplug

on 110th, where we fished the gutter
for bottle caps to gamble with—Pepsi, Orange Cream.
Sent to bed early, we crouched behind walls

as if walls could shelter, world rocking under fire.
Listening in, we gnawed fingernails
to nubs, beamed flashlights at shadows, heard

our mothers coughing under clouds of Lucky Strikes.

La Guerre et La Paix

Pablo Picasso, Stone Chapel, Musée National, Vallauris, France

I

On the south wall of the chapel,
a man tramples skeletons, hauls
a sack of skulls—
stone slashed in blood

that deep vermilion found
in caves at Font-de-Gaume, Lascaux,
that coldness you'd expect below ground
here too, but marked by sword not spear.

It was the year Picasso met his anger at war
in shades of brown, drew
a man hurling a brew
of corkscrew bacteria,

drew hooves crushing books
in fire. Yet near the chapel door
Picasso drew that man stopped dead
before a giant brandishing a shield—

on the shield, a dove, and hidden
in the dove, the smile of a woman,
Françoise Gilot, who told Picasso
                    You must paint peace.

I won't he cried, *there is no reason—*

II

The guidebook tells she raised
her voice, held his brush like a knife, said
*You must embrace the other wall,
there's nothing else to do*

with dark but ravish it
in yellow, green, and blue, show
the piper, owl, a child who ploughs
the sea, a baby at her mother's breast,

and so Picasso relented, turned
resistance into truce,

drew a woman reading poems under a vine,
children dancing on the ocean's skin—   Still

all face a headless man, a mortal thigh.

RELEASE

After Anselm Kiefer's Fitzcarraldo, 2010

Hand over mouth, misshapen fingers
spotted brown, she stares at faults not hers
the woods before her riven by roots
studded as hobnail boots
roots with mud encrusted arms
with ash with thorns—

the way it was, eyes drawn into routes
to survival, underground toeholds the uprooted
seek to weather grief—   brittle frost unbroken
and she, frozen between splintered echoes, spies
an *Aschenblume* rupturing umber
young roots in ashes the forest revives
just when she thought there would be no end
to being icebound—

At the Paper Sculpture Exhibit

Bergamot Station Art Galleries, Santa Monica, CA

The world inside a paper bag.
The bag set on its side—
The bag a set of surfaces
containing life arrested,
containing life scissored
with care, the hollow
like a pastoral inside a hollow
sugared egg.
                    Imagine
being there—   the tiny civilization,
placid green lawn, park bench,
tree's shadow dependent on the fiction
imposed. No complication. No blight.
And there, the paper girl, the paper boy,
the paper puppy no larger than a rosebud.

Inside the bag, no manic
wind, no soil, no rows, no rule. The artist tames
the tree, the dog, the boy, the girl, the still
life held within the paper walls—

DRAGONFLY

Beware the dragonfly! No fool fragile
as old lace, that devil's needle
stitches lips, stings fingertips, scores

names of those who don't obey
on air. Some dare the double-winged
to land on arms, the darter's eyes

ravenous. But not for us—the lies
of folklore harmless. No match for lies
the dragons snarl. Hear them blare

You're either with us or against us.
Catch your breath—they're spooling names
on the no-fly list

while orange aerialists skim pools
for larvae—whir of color, no rumble
of planes commanded to bumble the ballet—

more likely Basho's *Crimson pepper pod*
appeasing ghosts, devouring virus-laden prey,

a dragon dipping down to find a blade
of grass to perch on.

AN ENCOUNTER WITH CY TWOMBLY AT THE WHITNEY

Cy Twombly, 50 Years of Works on Paper, May 2005

I don't think of them as scribbles—what critics call my signature.

I scumble alphabets,
        sly under
                tangles of sea kelp, flowers floating
                on the skin of a pond—   black and scarlet daubs,

score a loose calligraphy on surfaces— *Awake a moment /*
                                        Mind dreams again /
                                        Red rose black edged

and this *As long as you have*

I layer text, bury pencil curls with crimson oil stick, smudge out
what's there,
        runes transcribed in plum

weighted *dark purple,* and here, *of the* cloaked in ink
        I could hear sinking through paper's tooth.

I don't think of them as abstract—

        more improvisation, bricolage, fragments
        a way to overlay allusion
        find my way as the red sun
        burns away
        too soon

Try folding the wind to leave a landscape torn. Yes,
the scribbles, rubbings, scrapings,
        clashes of energy on field after field, the *Ides of March.*
This is the hand—

Long Odds

Where cholla meets Mojave aster,
stems raveled by hikers she ignores,
the tortoise shovels
a shallow basin—   slow
work before she knows the hole will hold
what she has come to leave.

She settles in silence and starts to lay.
White orbs, wet and ripe, pile
on each other like ping pong balls,
progeny curled in paper shells; Empty,
she showers sand over the nest, smooths it
with broad front paws and rests;
her eyes glaze over, seem not to see.

Some genetic map instructing, she turns
toward her burrow, escapes the task,
escapes the scent of rats, coyotes, skunks,
who lurk to lick her eggs dry—

DOES IT HURT?

My son stands riveted
where men in rubber boots
and yellow aprons sprayed
with blood lop heads
off quivering fish,
toss entrails
at the toes of milling gulls.
The child stares, eyes
mirroring the kill, and asks me
Does it hurt?

               I face away,
rehearse the way I'll offer cash
for fish, explain ecology,
the food chain, need,
while in a bucket near his feet
fish heads float, lips apart and blue.

SPORT

               Out of cover
we come to the edge
of the lake.
                    In a red
canoe, a man and a woman.

The woman watches the man love
his gun, stroke its glint with his palm.
He lines up his eye, looks down

the barrel and shoots; pellets dent
          the sheer surface. The decoy lists.

The woman raises her
paddle, back strokes. Ravens slice
the sky wheeling and cawing. Black

flies stitch the air.
                    The man fires. I wanted

the lake silent, wanted this fall of black
flies. Who tease the man who shoots.

          Noon. Water a pewter page. Lonesome
Lake, breadth held in a cradle

of thickets. Shots tremble
the water, the captured
moment, ourselves in cross-hairs—

AT THUNDER HOLE

Acadia National Park

It was water
        we came to hear
                that roar

of soaring crests
        blotting the horizon
                the light

layered
        that morning
                mother-of-pearl

the blue heave
        hissing and breaking
                littering the air

the trail peopled then
        the wave lashing
                sweeping in

a child
        the wash heavy
                entangling

arms and legs
        too slow
                and the divers

who felt the wave
        dragging the undertow
                could find nothing

and the fish who felt the child
        flailing against seaweed
                could do nothing

the light that morning falling like gauze

POSTCARD FROM PLACE OF REFUGE

Pu'uhonua o Honaunau National Historic Park, HI

A gull tugs at a crab stuck fast in wrack—
tideline given and taken over coral shelves
where the dead shift in shells
as water licks the sickle-
shaped cove
and saffron finch and mynah peck
at color, score the depression
where turquoise stains the roots
of fuchsia and photinia—

No clues explain the hue,
the blossom fall.
No turquoise under pili.
No turquoise under makaloa.

We question the odor. *Herbicide*
the ranger says. *We protect the natives.*

A NATURAL PHENOMENON

*Semelparous: a species that reproduces once a lifetime, then dies.
Caña is a semelparous bamboo.*

Science can't explain how it happens—
perhaps some trait of memory
to carry on.

Caña blooms not seen in more than sixty
years, tilt top-heavy brooms.
No semelparity is clean or orderly—

We're here where *Caña* bow in unison
across 200,000 acres, tier the Patagonian
forest floor with seeds—   a feast for common

long-tailed mice who stuff and multiply by ten
or more. Trekking, we hear ruckus.
Like toes scampering on cellophane.

Seeds split and crackle. Soon hungry long-tails
flee the forest for the towns,
hover under wood piles, homes, bear hantavirus

close enough to kill. How the death-dance
of the Caña tips the risk to us who have become
the long-tails' last chance.

THREE

SUSPENSION

I

This is a truth for you to sort, my father,
born in Brooklyn, not born in Brooklyn,
wanting to ward off— what?

You signed me up for school, signed
your birthplace slanted cursive—just a swerve
in a new dance, no loss

helping dislocation disappear. You, my father,
who could spin the tale of "Ali Baba
and the Forty Thieves" for forty nights,

could never tell your own. How the music
of America pulsed between your toes, even
as you heaved in steerage, boy of eleven

leaving Romania, holes in shoes, coins
stuffed in socks with raveled threads.

II

You quickly fitted your tongue to English, sang
Open Sesame in pure American.
Nobody questioned it, the fiction flawless

as the glass of Lower New York Bay belies
its silt. Countless times you crossed
The Narrows on the ferry, casting

overboard the pogroms, bolted
doors, your brother's death, wanting,
like Crane, to build *high*

Over the chained bay waters Liberty.

III

Now the Verrazano spans the bay,
giant harp, steel strings caught
by rivets big as wrists, harmony of cables

playing in the wind, and you, my father,
on a platform high above the swells, cut
ribbons opening the bridge you helped design.

Imagine my not knowing
you weren't born in Brooklyn
until after you died!

IV

I was a child blanketed in the back seat
of the Plymouth. You taught me stress
and strain are not the same,

how strain is part of any bridge,
is always there; but stress deforms,
causes heave and buckle of a span.

When I was six you sketched a bridge
suspended over water, cantilevers,
trusses, beams, told me

you could build a bridge to bear a load,
to sway in wind yet anchor
firm. That bridge still holds.

for Stanley Steven Haendel 1911-1964

THE ASTRONOMER

Out at midnight watching
sky, he hopes clouds will split, wants
auroras, dancing girls
in silk pajamas, waterfalls
of azure ribbons through the gauze,

recalls black nights, a child
in the Caucasus, belly empty, bowl
of sky without a star, nights
flailing in sheets, body
waiting to fall, his windows
rattling, strangers at the gate.

                        On the train,
his hands, so cold, held tight to steam-
ship tickets to America. Through the pane,
he watched the Black Sea
distance, his far village, shooting
stars a glow across the dome.

CHROMATIC ALPHABET

In Vilna, dark and light embrace.
She clutches words wrapped in a prayer,
reaches Ellis Island holding close

to Russian, Polish, Yiddish— *Tumbalalaika*
in her ear, she'd make a place. It was before
that man at immigration cleansed her

name to Lepon, shouted Lejpunski
for the umpteenth time,
an uproar for her pride, her name,

but composure kicked in
slipping off her lips delicious as a poem.
She excised her raspy *k,* tucked reluctance

under new perfection, diction precise
as a San Franciscan bustling with caprice
down Market street, counting bliss

in coppers, nickels, dimes earned
at the dry goods store where she kissed
a man headed to Alaska for gold, sold

him overalls, and convinced him to stay—
folded history in denim, days she rode
in steerage wedged between the wary

and the fevered in the hold, years she lost
inflection, only nasality surviving.
It was her way—

for Goldie Lepon Ginsberg, 1879–1972

ACCIDENT, MARYLAND

Arrived in *Accident* by accident—
deep dent in the road rent by winter
rage, spring flood

spilling over leaving skins of ice
on asphalt. We stop. No reason but loss
of direction. *So where's the map*

you shout as though what brought
us to a halt is someone's fault.

No blood on the shoulder of the road.
No skid on the bend—yet I feel

that sting of nettles
brushed by chance, blind reach

into a blackberry patch in search
of sweetness, love.

OMELET

I hear you beating eggs,
the wire whisk, a tambourine
against the bowl.
I lie in bed
so lazy after love,
the sense of you still warm
between my legs,
I'm not hungry yet.
You return
and touch my skin,
your fingers strong
with garlic, lavender,
and cheese, aromas
sure to tease me from
serenity
to insist we yield to food.

Edward Weston's *Pepper*

Pepper No. 30, *1930, Gelatin Silver Print*

Waiting for decay, he spoke
quietly of ripening, of piquancy,
of longing for the right
exposure—

He set her upright
her cap lit
in grisaille, his eye
pressed to her skin like a palm
against each cell, his eye

brushing the slope of her
flesh

I will wait for
shadows to fall shallow on her
folds, he mused. *The failing light*

will follow her
stem   her neck   her
smooth geography   before
I close in close

to sight her drooping
shoulder   her withering
haunch   before I tilt my lens
before I take her.

Help Wanted: Bra Fitter

Escalator bound for second. Bras at rest.
Empty cups clamor *Fill me*. The job
with the perfect fit. Think of it
as artistry, a sculptor's possibilities

in the right hands, a way to lift the loose
and flaccid, mold the folds and creases

into maiden form. You're sixty-one,
laid off and miffed—
twenty-six years. No severance.
No frills. No lace. You need a lift.

The interviewer elbows figure eights
of hanging bras, a dance

of pink and bone. Think lace, not homespun—
When her palm gently strokes your worn
herringbone suit, you swallow the ache—
your empty fridge, your empty tank.

Face it. Don't expire. You're broke.
Think tooth and claw. You need a break,

some firm support. Embrace the chance
to *name the problem that has no name.*
So you ask—What's the pay?
Health insurance? 401 K?

REPRIEVE

A sparrow strikes the window
Dead?
Ounce of down and hollow bone
still warm.

You stroke its head; feathers
flutter from your palm, falter
on a branch, limb too thin
for life support. Cat paces, rubs your shin,
her fur in spikes.

I hear your steady breath,
remember flutters
in your heart, skipped
beats you laugh away,
a muscle out of tune you say,
cascades of modern jazz.

So quiet this afternoon,
the only sound
your hand erasing air
as if to send the sparrow
on its way, my fear diminished
grace notes summoned
as the wings extend.

REVELATION

It's impossible to live without skin
coding us, not us, them, not them, so much
depends upon geography and gene,
the map of haplotypes a palette rich
in melanin; only the measure thins
or fattens choice. Why then can more bring less,
vermillion blush the same on opaline
flesh or sable? I look at how your face
and mine wear scuff marks, familiar dark hair
white and rough to touch, your neck glistening
ebony, mine shining pale amber, race
no longer fencing families' embrace—
how age and care have made an opening
allowing light, bright color at the core.

SCHOODIC SONNET

After Tangled Roots, *photograph by Ruth Ginsberg-Place*

In the photograph—roots braided
over rock shards, over mud, wood
stretching arms to hug the ground
so we are drawn into the bed

of mulch as if kneeling to smell the earth,
to touch the velvet of wet bark.
Our eye moves down the trail to birch
leaves tattered under foot marks—

deer, coyote, raccoon, human
who tread where dense clouds
crumble under weight of sun and sullen
fog can shutter sense—   the form
drawing the mind from shadows
into sight—   roots knotted as kin.

Impulse of the Hand

Taiaroa Head, Otago Peninsula, NZ

On a slope above the sea a woman draws
her scarf around her as the land
draws to itself the surf's shoulders.

She draws on a stone pillow
hand singing in a linen covered book
above a nest of spoonbills, sand

scribbling a shallow lip along the rock
ledge where a shearwater dives for cuttlefish.
The woman slips pens into a pocket

notices the black-rimmed eye of a gull
orange as the plastic fence that rims
a preservation plot. Drawing still—

each breath scythed through skin
an echo of the swell and crash
the long exhale, she who praises, raises pen.

CUT BLOOMS

Something about the shout
of color sharpens
sense, flash
of yellow, black-
eyed susans
on her kitchen table, fresh,
unstinting in their gaze.

After a week, once buoyant
blossoms, limp,
nod at no one, drowse
the way my mother nods
and stares at air,

whispers, *why have you come
alone, left the children
home, with whom?*

My children? They're middle-aged,
fathers themselves, her first great grandson
going on fourteen, feet
bigger than his dad's.

I watch my mother
pluck petals from a daisy's head, murmur
loves me, loves me not.

Not the only way
to pull a flower apart.

THE PAINTER AT NINETY-ONE

Her eyes fatigue. Ghosts dance
around the rods and cones, wash halos
over reds and blues
as if the dazzle of an ordinary day
were singed. On the easel, flecks
of paint blink on and off
like fireflies; split vision's
usual, a trick the body plays in age
and yet—she hungers for an image,
marvels how Matisse, too ill
to paint, cut papers, indigo, ecru,
magenta, green, collaged
improvisations, *Jazz.*

She squeezes pigment on a sheet of glass
as though her eyes remember
how to harness light, cerulean blue
the hue of ocean near
her childhood home, and ochre,
sheen on ripe tomatoes.
Fingers bent as winter twigs, she blends
the yellow into crimson, gilds
the grasses of a meadow tangerine
and shapes a woman standing
at an easel, holding brush to air.

Habañera

We dismantle her
house, divide the things
we've lived among, the books
and photographs, lift Chagall's
Musician off its hook, unplug
the stereo, collect librettos,
1936, Caruso at the Met.

Small things speak up
emptying
her boxes full of pills
the special phone
with giant numerals, its shrill
ring, two hearing aids,
her teeth, the upper partial
resting in a blue plastic case.

We dismantle the bed
remove the rail, the kind
you use to keep a child
from falling in the night,
find her glasses folded
on the table. She always left
them open, ready, ear pieces
jutting from the frame—

Yellow jonquils glow
before the mantel mirror.
Her friend Minna brought them,
knowing it would change nothing,
mother, singing behind the rhythm
of a Carmen aria, becoming eggshell,
loose in her big chair, no longer knowing
Minna but loving Carmen, loving yellow.

CLEANING OUT HER CLOSET

My mother's mink came back
to life, that trapped body,

wary, that silence she wore
before my father

could afford her need,
that softness I strained

to touch   and there
I was   empty twice—

BLUES FOR DOROTHY

Leaving her bones she flew—a loose balloon
between the eucalyptus
winding north. She knew distances
indigo and azure, knew color, knew

the yellow light leaving   furious
as any hyacinth blue she could make
flare—   knew quivers, knew

the body after self evaporates, mingles
with shadow as it rises up in air.
Only bone burns to silver, my brother says—

She could be anywhere   gathering
the bright   a shape assembling
itself in a sea of blues—

THE CONCHOLOGIST AND THE SHOEMAKER

The blind professor's no stranger to seeing
the terrain rocky, his boots wearing thin—
what needs repair he says, *the tear hidden*
in the sole below my arch, skin splitting

where my feet have swelled with age, the right close
around my ankle, the fit less good, the smell
somehow off, more of sweat than leather. Tell
me—might the odor come from coast sea moss?

The shoemaker strokes his chin and looks him
in the eye that glisters, says *I'll stretch them*
half a size and smooth the saddle—the smell?
the shells you study, sir, their sea-salt film.

The blind professor rubs his fingers on
the boot's hide, traces seams and cuts, searches
for clues, says *look, this torn selvage reaches*
inside like sea-worn specimens of Conus

litteratus. The shoemaker slides his thumb
over instep sweat-polished warm, feels the last,
sees scratches don't penetrate the surface.
Wax will seal the skin he says, *amber cream.*

But the color asks the blind professor
will it change? I love the deep tone, I fear
it's faded some. I want the glow of sea,
no yellowing no darkening, no premature

unraveling, the stitches strong as gut
for scrambling over algae-slicked rocks
below tide line, where the mollusks
hide. The shoemaker leans closer, grins, *this cut*

of boot, grooved on the sole, grips sand.
The blind professor rubs his palms together,
laughs, *I need my boots in every weather—*
so much I've yet to see with these hands.

Alice Neel Speaks

Self-Portrait, *1980, Oil on Canvas,*
Smithsonian American Art Museum, Washington, D.C.

My face is gone. My pubic hair
is gone— a brush stroke
and I can change all that
but not the truth.

A brush stroke and a face hides
in a well of shadows. It's the face
that places nakedness in focus, strips
veneer, releases flesh from armature.

Like Gogol's Chichikov, I collect souls,
fix them alla prima as they expose
themselves. Ha! I relish nakedness,
each grimace alive with fire.

I preface the loss of beauty with glee,
tease folds of my abundancy with rose.
I'm round with eighty, have the will
to paint myself, appraisal open to the bone.

Here I sit in my blue striped chair.
In my hand, a brush, a rag. More than gesture,
the milky blue sculpts my face, erases
creases from my jaw. I split the surface

of the floor with orange warming lime,
colors of lust and excess below bare feet.
Naked in the glass, I survey my legs spread
forcefully apart, calf muscle softened

with mauve, belly folded like a petal, curves
of peach and mango paint connecting flesh
and self. A brush stroke and I can change
all that, but not the truth.

RESILIENCE

In the expanse of birch and maple
behind my house, leaves are letting go
opening the distance, though
the trail's still cunning, the deep hollows
hidden by October's brimming fall.

Walking in the woods with Simon trying
to pull free from his leash, I lose my
footing, trip over exposed roots and find
myself sprawled in leaf litter, foliage
thick with what lives buried where my body

now lies lucky, net of gold and salmon
mulch, a cradle for the old woman
I am growing into. I sink gratefully, reach
a branch to help me up, let Simon lick my smile—
No margin for misstep now.

I remember last winter tackling the icy trail uphill
to get the mail, woods crossed with broken arms
of storm-thrown oaks and hemlocks. Perhaps
that cracked ankle and the crawl for help
were warnings to tread carefully, but why—

my body still wanting to come
out in the sun, to smell the loam of my own
soil, full with mushrooms this fall, oysters
and parasols driving upward
through decaying ferns.

About the Author

Edythe Haendel Schwartz is the author of *Exposure*, Finishing Line Press, 2007, a nominee for the California Book Award. Her poem "A Natural Phenomenon" won first prize in the 2012 Friends of Acadia Poetry competition, and her poem "Resist" was a winner in Persimmon Tree's 2011 Western States Poetry Competition. In 2006 and 2008, Edythe was awarded grants for residencies at The Vermont Studio Center. Her poems appear widely in journals and anthologies, including *Calyx, Cave Wall, California Quarterly, PMS, Poetica, Natural Bridge, Earth's Daughters, Poet Lore, Pearl, Sierra Nevada Review, Persimmon Tree, Potomac Review, JAMA, Hawaii Pacific Review, Vermont Literary Review, Cider Press Review, Runes, Spillway, Thema,* and *Water-Stone,* among others. Now retired from the faculty, Department of Child Development, California State University, Sacramento, Edythe is a visual artist as well as a poet. She lives with her husband, Sy, in Davis, CA, where she swims daily with the Davis Aquatic Masters and dances with Pamela Trokanski's Dance Workshop's Second Wind group.

Other Recent Titles from Mayapple Press:

Sarah Busse, *Somewhere Piano,* 2012
        Paper, 72pp, $14.95 plus s&h
        ISBN 978-1-936419-13-5
Betsy Johnson-Miller, *Fierce This Falling,* 2012
        Paper, 72pp, $14.95 plus s&h
        ISBN 978-1-936419-12-8
William Heyen, *Straight's Suite for Craig Cotter and Frank O'Hara,* 2012
        Paper, 86pp, $14.95 plus s&h
        ISBN 978-1-936419-11-1
Lydia Rosner, *The Russian Writer's Daughter,* 2012
        Paper, 104pp, $15.95 plus s&h
        ISBN 978-1-936419-10-4
John Palen, *Small Economies,* 2012
        Paper, 58pp, $13.95 plus s&h
        ISBN 978-1-936419-09-8
Susan Azar Porterfield, *Kibbe,* 2012
        Paper, 62pp, $14.95 plus s&h
        ISBN 978-1-936419-08-1
Susan Kolodny, *After the Firestorm,* 2011
        Paper, 62pp, $14.95 plus s&h
        ISBN 978-1-936419-07-4
Eleanor Lerman, *Janet Planet,* 2011
        Paper, 210pp, $16.95 plus s&h
        ISBN 978-1-936419-06-7
George Dila, *Nothing More to Tell,* 2011
        Paper, 100pp, $15.95 plus s&h
        ISBN 978-1-936419-05-0
Sophia Rivkin, *Naked Woman Listening at the Keyhole,* 2011
        Paper, 44pp, $13.95 plus s&h
        ISBN 978-1-936419-04-3
Stacie Leatherman, *Stranger Air,* 2011
        Paper, 80pp, $14.95 plus s&h
        ISBN 978-1-936419-03-6
Mary Winegarden, *The Translator's Sister,* 2011
        Paper, 86pp, $14.95 plus s&h
        ISBN 978-1-936419-02-9

For a complete catalog of Mayapple Press publications, please visit our website at *www.mayapplepress.com.* Books can be ordered direct from our website with secure on-line payment using PayPal, or by mail (check or money order). Or order through your local bookseller.